# Happy Has Always Been The Plan

INCLUDING VERSE BY
VERSE COMMENTARY OF SONG OF SOLOMON

CHRIS RAY

Library of Congress Control Number:        2020923054

HARDBACK:          978-1-953791-51-1
PAPERBACK:         978-1-953791-50-4
EBOOK:             978-1-953791-52-8

Ordering Information:

For orders and inquiries, please contact:
1-888-404-1388
www.goldtouchpress.com
book.orders@goldtouchpress.com


Printed in the United States of America

# CONTENTS

# CHAPTER 1

## *Why?*

Why is there so much misery? Why so many suicides? Why so much pain and heartache? What are we missing? Wait a minute! Why are some people happy? Why do some people have joy and a peace that passes all understanding? What have they found? What is different about their lives?

Some people are happy because that has always been the plan. I taught my five kids that if you are not happy, you are doing something wrong. It really is that simple. People want to argue that fact and it still remains that it is that simple. Some people are happy, most are not. Let's see if we can move to the happy crowd. Know upfront that it is your choice. You actually will choose whether you will be happy or not.

The happy crowd starts with God. Without God there really is no lasting happiness and joy. Our society uses drugs, alcohol and sex to bring momentary relief. The problem is we wake up in the morning. That's right. We wake up and the world is still there. People still mistreat us, use and abuse us, find fault with us etc. That makes us angry. Things don't work out the way we want. That makes us mad. And then there is the body thing. It keeps getting older and falling apart. We really are running out of time. That alone can be very frustrating.

Is this all there is? Will the world never revolve around us? You know the answer to that. Of course not! The world will never revolve around you because it is not about you. Never has been and never will be. You didn't create this world for your purpose. You didn't even create yourself. You never decided to be born. You just found yourself here. You didn't pick anything: Not parents, nation, neighbors, teachers, not even what language you would originally speak. Welcome to the world as it is, not as you would necessarily want it.

Given this world is like it is, how can we be happy? What makes us think we can be happy? Why is it we even have trouble defining "happy"? There are people that are happy, so that means it is possible. Even better, in John 10:10 Jesus tells us: The thief cometh not, but for to steal, and to kill, and to destroy: I am come *that they might have life, and that they might have* it more abundantly. Wow! He actually came to give us life and not just life, but an abundant life. That means happy, joyous, free. That means experiencing fuller, richer, good, wholesome emotions. That means loving and being loved. Living life as it was intended to be lived. Happy has always been the plan.

The problem is us. We have a better plan. We know what will make us happy or so we think. We don't need this God stuff. Or maybe some kind of God that does what we want and not what he wants. Why doesn't God just leave us alone? The answer to that question is a real eye opener. **God doesn't leave us alone because he loves us.** Let that sink in. He loves us too much to just leave us alone.

God created heaven, and earth, the sea and all that therein is. He created it for his purpose. That means we were created for his purpose. We are all messed up and have all sinned. We have all gone against God. The soul that sinneth, it shall die. The word death means separation. This means we must be separated from a totally holy, pure God. We need a savior. Someone to save us from our sins. God sent his son into the world to live a sinless life (so he didn't have to die) and then voluntarily die for us. Jesus paid the price for all of our sins. Jesus became sin for us. He died for us. Then note the simple guide on page 75 to help get you started.

People want a God that will do as they please. The problem with that is that there is a way that seems right to us, but it ends in death. Remember, God doesn't let us do anything we want because he loves us. Jesus is the God that created everything. Then he showed what love is by dying for us.

All of our emotions are what enrich our lives. If we don't have emotions, then we have a very shallow life. We saw this early on. We love our emotions. Unfortunately, that becomes our first problem. We twist and pervert the good emotions that were given to enrich our lives. They then become the very things that ruin our lives.

Pleasure and all the feelings that go with it are a gift from God. He made us to experience pleasure. He gave us sex. Not only does it keep the human race multiplying, it is also extremely pleasurable. He made us long for affection because he knew how much we would like it. He knew natural affection would make our neighborhoods better. We would help each other. We would draw close to each other. We would experience love and give love. Our lives would be much fuller.

He knew there would be those that abuse this. He told us upfront not to covet our neighbor's goods or wife. He told us not to lie. He saw that we needed a few guidelines to ensure that the emotions would not be wrong. He gave us anger to help us manage our own lives. We realize that there are things that should not happen. There are things that people do that are not right. This should make us angry. Our inner being seems to call out: stop it! Of course, we abused the very emotions he gave to enrich us. That's why we needed a savior.

Jesus didn't just come to save us and then leave us alone. I repeat, he came to give us the best lives we could have. He gave us his spirit to be with us 24/7. He told us we were never alone. He repeatedly told us not to fear. How's that working for us? Fear is also a great emotion. It prevents us from many mistakes, bad decisions etc. Fear gives us the opportunity to be brave. We are exhilarated when we are brave and courageous. Fear teaches us to avoid those things that would hurt us. It is why we don't stick our hands in the fire.

However, (I know you are ahead of me on this) we tend to twist and pervert this emotion as well. Fear is to help us, not paralyze us. Imagine a life without fearing people, places or things that we have no control over. We might even be happy. Yea.

I know what my biggest problem is. Number one problem: I think I think pretty good. This lurks behind or sometimes in front of about everything I do. This happens when you have an idea and I have an idea, mine is better. It stems from selfishness. This one massive flaw has caused me more pain, challenges, problems, relationship damages etc. This is why I didn't listen to good advice. This is why I made the same mistakes over and over. This is why I am a slow learner. Once I saw this as my flaw, I could get better.

Many people will not read this book because they know better. They are miserable, but they feel they know more than anyone else. They think they have done pretty well with the cards they have been dealt. Again, the problem is selfishness. We are consumed with looking out for ourselves. We find it hard to believe that someone else has a better idea. We really feel that we are the ones who have to make sure we are ok. I am amazed at how many people say they have to learn to love themselves. There are not many statements that are more selfish than that. FYI, nowhere does God ever tell us to love ourselves. He tells us to love him and love others.

No matter how many times we prove we don't know best, we still trust ourselves. The problem is that we were made to trust someone else. We were specifically made to not know the future. That's right. We were made to not know the future. Look at the astrologists, mystics, fortune tellers and all the rest of the people that make a lot of money trying to tell others the future. Heads up! If you knew the future, you would be God. If things always happened the way you wanted, you would be God. Isn't it strange how much time and money are put towards playing God?

This is where it gets good. God said TRUST HIM. He knew we would not understand what he was doing so he specifically wrote Proverbs 3:5,6 telling us to trust him and lean not to our own understanding, but rather in all things acknowledge that he is God and he will direct our path. This flies against our selfishness. We don't want to trust anyone but ourselves.

It is our choice. We can believe God and trust God and stop playing God. He knows the future and has all the power. I mean think about it. He created everything. Every star you can see as well as every star you can't see. He knows what will happen and has proved it repeatedly. He tells us up front and then explains who else could tell you up front. In the bible, he called people by name a hundred years before they were born. He told the Israelites that they would be in captivity in Babylon for 70 years. He foretold Jesus would be born in Bethlehem etc. He knows, you don't. He also knows you don't. So, he said to trust him. It is that simple.

By now we are beginning to see that it is not complicated. It really is simple. It is also available to everyone. It is always our choice. We can choose to believe the record that God gave of his son. This is the starting point. He gave us the bible to tell us everything we need to know. The main holdup to happiness is us. **God won't force us to be blessed**. God won't force us to be great. He will enable us.

We don't have to listen to God. We don't have to read his word. He gives us everything we need but we don't have to take it. We can be as miserable as we want. It is always our choice. Ironically, we usually know the right thing to do. If we just do the next right thing, we are fine. The problem is we always have the choice. We can choose to not listen. We can choose to not go where and when we know we should. We can say "I know I should but…" I now realize that when I didn't do what I knew I should, I lost the blessing.

If I didn't go on that men's retreat, I lost the blessing. If I didn't go to that conference, I lost the blessing. If I didn't go to church, I lost the blessing. If I didn't go to that funeral, I lost the blessing. ETC., ETC., ETC. The real problem is that we never even know the blessings we missed. Our lives were meant to be full, happy and joyous. That has always been the plan. We don't even know all the blessings intended for us. We missed them because we did not do the next right thing.

Also note: we try to explain a blessing we got to someone else and realize they won't see it like we did. We can't get the same blessing through someone else's experience. We can be blessed by them, but it is not the same. The original blessing cannot be passed on. God intended it that way. He begs us to do the next right thing so that we may be fully blessed.

One particular book of the bible opens the door very well. The Song of Solomon emphasizes the relationship God desires with each of us. When we think about relationships, we realize that they are the source of our most wonderful emotions. Relationships are for love. Relationships bring us feelings of joy, togetherness, tenderness, gentleness, peace, security, stability, laughter and hope. Yes, looking at children and grandchildren is meant to bring us hope. God wants us to have great relationships because he loves us.

I am reminded of a wedding reception for one of my children. At one point all five of them were on the dance floor. They were all laughing, loving, in good clean fun. I found myself sitting at a table watching them and I realized I was smiling. I thoroughly enjoyed watching my kids have a wonderful time. **God reminded me that he smiles when I'm laughing**. That is so good. This is what God intended. Happy has always been his plan for us.

Knowing that relationships can also be the source of our greatest hurts, pains, and heartaches, he gives us instructions throughout his word to help us. My platform is "God Wrote It to You". His word is for each and every one of us. He didn't just write to the preachers, priests and bishops. God wrote it to you! Because he loves you.

His word shows some of the benefits and some of the pitfalls. There are things to look for in our lives. There are ways to improve our relationships. Our relationship with God himself is the place to start. What follows is a verse by verse commentary on the Song of Solomon. In it, God shows how he takes care of it all. We trust him with our lives.

God brought me an illustration regarding relationships and life in general. This changed my life. This enabled me to think before I made a horrible mistake. I realized that I have no control over people, places and things. I cannot change them. I am not responsible for them. I am responsible for my own actions and reactions. I turned my life and my will over to God. I told him to do whatever he wanted and help me to accept that. He gave me what I now call "The Movie".

# CHAPTER 2

## The Movie

I am not very big or important, but I'm about all I ever think about. When I realized that I had a starring role in a major motion picture, I was thrilled. It is the movie of my life. God is the producer, director and the writer. I am just the actor. This changed everything. I realized that I have a part and I want to do it well. I quit griping because I want to keep my job as the lead actor.

As I go through life, I sometimes hear the director yell cut. I have messed up or missed the point of the scene. The director shows what I need to change and we go on because I trust the director. I didn't write the script so sometimes I am asked to do something I didn't expect or want to do. That's ok because I trust the writer. I asked a friend of mine in the film industry what the producer does. He said the producer gathers all the resources. Everything I have in my life and all the people around me are gathered for me by the producer.

I found that much like a regular movie, those who have a speaking part are important in some way. There are actors in the background, but without a speaking part, they are there mostly for flavor or ambiance. I have come to really enjoy those who have a speaking part in the movie of my life. I have found repeatedly that those with speaking parts are adding to my joy. I begin to see that the producer did a great job bringing them to the movie. The script put me where I could be blessed by them. The director is constantly trying to help me deal with them correctly. He wants the scene to be worthwhile. Ironically, so do I. So I listen.

This movie has remarkably changed my life. I spent several years talking with myself in the third person. Something happens and I think "Chris didn't like that" or "Chris didn't see that coming". This was followed many times by the thought "How should Chris respond to this" or something along those lines. When I was wrong in the response, I could almost hear the director yelling "cut". I got to the point where I would ask the director upfront when I didn't know what to do. He likes that because that is his job.

I get to see some parts of the script ahead of time but mostly it is as it happens. I now see life as a gigantic adventure. I can't wait to see what happens. So many times I didn't like what was happening as it happened. Sometimes, afterwards, I would see how it had to happen that way for something else (that I liked) to happen. I began to see that God really does know best. I should trust him. That means I can't ever gripe or complain. I also noticed that nothing made me mad anymore. Where I live, work, play etc. is all part of the writing, producing and directing. It works well because I trust the writer, producer and director. I don't know what the movie is called. I guess how I live will be a determining factor. The title goes on when I leave this earth.

Imagine a life where you don't get angry or frustrated about anything that you cannot change. Weather comes to mind for most people. When you think about it, what control do you have? Basically, the only thing you can change is you. Ahhhh, now we are getting somewhere. Enter the Song Of Solomon.

# CHAPTER 3

## *What's Your Purpose?*

Why are you here? What is the reason for your life?

Why are we all here? Good questions.

Several years ago, I took my boys and some other people up to Michigan on a ski trip. Midway through the day, the chairlift I was riding in stopped half way up the mountain. I had normally been riding with one or more of the people in my group, but this particular ride was just me and a man with a ski- patrol jacket on. After dangling in the chilly breeze for several minutes, I asked him what his particular function was. He replied that he was the man in charge of evacuating the chairlifts in the event of a breakdown. We both laughed at the irony of that. It then occurred to me that I was looking at a golden opportunity.

As the cold air whistled by, I said "Mike, what's your purpose in life? Why are you here?" He thought a moment, then mentioned that that was a good question. He said he thought that he was here to help people. I asked him to consider for a moment what would be his purpose if this chairlift plummeted to the ground and he was a quadriplegic.

That is interesting isn't it? What is your purpose if you not only can't help others, you can't even help yourself? Now we all know there are quadriplegics in this world. What is their purpose? Good question huh? It seems it might take someone like God to answer that. He does.

In the bible God tells us that a lawyer asked Jesus what the number one thing God wanted from us was. Mark 12:28 ²⁸And one of the scribes came, and having heard them reasoning together, and perceiving that he had answered them well, asked him, Which is the first commandment of all? ²⁹And Jesus answered him, The first of all the commandments is, Hear, O Israel; The Lord our God is one Lord: ³⁰And thou shalt love the Lord thy God with all thy heart, and with all thy soul, and with all thy mind, and with all thy strength: this is the first commandment.

The answer is that God wants us to love Him. That is why we are here. That is why we were made with a spirit, soul and body. The wonderful truth is that God made us to love Him. That is why we have free will. Without free will we would be chairs. Meaning that we would simply do what we were made to do. A chair is a chair. It will not be anything else. It cannot refuse to be a chair. It simply is a chair. A chair cannot love. It cannot choose anything. We can.

God gave us free will so that we would not be chairs. We can choose to love Him. Love is a choice. It is not something you fall into. That's why husbands are told to love their wives. God knows that it is a choice. He begs us to make the right choice. It would be no great thing for God to make us do something. He could have made us all keep all of the law all the time. But then it would not be us keeping it. It would be God making us keep it. We would have no choice. We would be like chairs. Every time you see a chair let it remind you that you are to love God. You are given a choice. Jesus says choose Him that you might have life, and have it more abundantly.

The absolutely wonderful news is that you can love God. Even if you have no arms or legs. You can love God. You can love God in sickness and in health, for better or for worse, forsaking all others...

Wait a minute. That sounds like the wedding vows. Yes it does. I'm glad you noticed. Why do people get married? They love each other. This brings us to the Song of Solomon. It's a story of love.

The Song of Solomon is a story of love between a king and a working girl. He is everything. She is just a nobody with nothing. She doesn't understand why but apparently he loves her.

This story is more than just a love story. The reason it is in the bible is because it is absolutely vital to us. Right here in the 21st century this book has meaning beyond our normal grasp. It is a supernatural book with mysteries that God explains to those who love Him. That is why God says it is the Song of Songs. More on that later.

In the book of the Revelation God refers to us as the bride of the lamb.

And there came unto me one of the seven angels which had the seven vials full of the seven last plagues, and talked with me, saying, Come hither, I will show thee the bride, the Lamb's wife.

The lamb is Jesus. He is referred to as the sacrificial lamb that was offered in atonement for our sin. Jesus is the innocent One. He never did anything wrong. He never sinned. God had said early on in Ezekiel 28

[4]Behold, all souls are mine; as the soul of the father, so also the soul of the son is mine: the soul that sinneth, it shall die.

The word "die" or "death" means separation. If anyone goes against God he must be separated from a totally holy, pure God. God will not tolerate any evil. He told Adam and Eve exactly that in the garden of Eden.

[16]And the LORD God commanded the man, saying, Of every tree of the garden thou mayest freely eat: [17]But of the tree of the knowledge of good

and evil, thou shalt not eat of it: for in the day that thou eatest thereof thou shalt surely die.

What God had done was give them a choice. They were not chairs. They could voluntarily choose to do what God wanted or they could refuse.

When they went against him, they died spiritually and began to die physically.

1Corinthians 15 21For since by man came death, by man came also the resurrection of the dead. 22For as in Adam all die, even so in Christ shall all be made alive.

So there you have it. God gives the test to see if man will choose to do what God would like or choose to do what he himself wants. When we love someone we want to do what they like. We want to please them.

Man made the wrong decision. He went against God and he paid the price. Now death is appointed to all men. And after death-the judgment.

Hebrews 9:27 And as it is appointed unto men once to die, but after this the judgment:

God knew that man would flunk the test. God knew that we would all have to be separated from Him. That is the natural result of giving us free will. We choose the wrong things. So what about God's plan for us to love Him and Him to love us. How would we ever get to the love, the eternity of bliss with our God. James 5:8 But God commendeth his love toward us, in that, while we were yet sinners, Christ died for us.

God Himself provided us the way out. He was not willing that any perish so God gave us His son to die in our place. Jesus never sinned, He never deserved to be separated from His father, He did not need to die. He voluntarily chose death for us. He died for us. He loved us so much that He died for us. Isn't that amazing? No one ever cared for us like Jesus.

Jesus took upon Himself the form of a man (we celebrate this at Christmas) and lived a sinless life so that He could die as a man. Two thousand years ago at the place of the skull Jesus paid the price for the sins of the world. He became the soul that died. When we choose to believe this record that God gave of His Son, God places us in Jesus on that cross. We are crucified with Jesus, nevertheless we live yet not us but Jesus who lives in us. The life that we now live we live by the faith of the Son of God who loved us and gave Himself for us. The just shall live by faith. We are justified by the blood of Jesus.

This is the background that God gives us showing us what real love is. For God so loved the world that He gave His only begotten son that whosoever believeth in Him should not perish but have everlasting life. This is not only the best known bible verse, it is the greatest example of love there is.

The question we should all ask is: Why would God love us? This is so foreign to the way we think. If we were constantly helping Him we could understand it. If we were always doing things that He likes, like telling Him how wonderful He is and spending time with Him, it would make sense. We could see Him loving us if we would hang on His every word, not able to hear enough from Him. The problem is that we are bringing nothing to the table. There are no good works, romantic stories, daring tales of how we gave up and sacrificed everything for Him. The truth is we pretty much have paid no attention to Him. We even rejected His advice. We pushed Him aside and boldly declared we would be our own person, making the best decisions we could no matter how flawed our thinking.

What is truly amazing is that, as our lives unfolded, we were proving ourselves wrong. The plans we made would turn out badly. The very things we thought would make us happy only served to bring us further into misery and heartache. Oddly enough, even when we looked around and saw that everyone else seemed to be in the same mess, we refused to change our course of action. For the most part we are so stubborn and stupid that we won't even accept His help as it is offered. Oh sure when we were really up against it we'd ask for His help, but just as soon as we were back on our feet we would run away from Him. We don't like to be told what to do.

He loved us still. He loved us when we were unlovable. This love was different than our love. We have trouble understanding this type of love. That's why He put the Song of Solomon in the bible. He knew we would need this explained. Oh wonder of wonders, once again He anticipated our need and gave us the answers He knew to the questions we should be directing to Him. Let's listen to what He says.

# CHAPTER 4

## The Greatest Song of All!

Chapter 1 For Song Of Solomon
¹The song of songs, which is Solomon's.

We read so fast that we miss it. Read it again. This is the song of songs. This is the song above all songs. This is the best song there is. This is the song of the King. Think of all the songs that have had you in tears. Have you ever listened to a song as the tears just rolled down your cheeks? You wanted to hear it over and over because it was somehow touching you in the deepest parts of your heart. It was wonderful.

This song is better. God, who cannot lie, says this song is better. God, who made all the emotions you experience says this song is better. Wouldn't you like to hear the greatest song there is? The best is offered, don't settle for less. God wouldn't tell you how good it can be if He didn't want you to have it. God will not withhold any good thing from those who love Him. This song is for you.
²Let him kiss me with the kisses of his mouth: for thy love is better than wine. ³Because of the savour of thy good ointments thy name is as ointment poured forth, therefore do the virgins love thee. ⁴Draw me, we will run after thee: the king hath brought me into his chambers: we will be glad and rejoice in thee, we will remember thy love more than wine: the upright love thee. ⁵I

am black, but comely, O ye daughters of Jerusalem, as the tents of Kedar, as the curtains of Solomon. [6]Look not upon me, because I am black, because the sun hath looked upon me: my mother's children were angry with me; they made me the keeper of the vineyards; but mine own vineyard have I not kept.

Love is the best emotion there is. It's better than getting high. We all have this incredibly strong desire to be loved. I remember as a teenager having this feeling of wanting someone to love. I felt that I had all this love to give to someone, if only there were a girl I could give it to. To love and be loved-I was catching my first glimpse of this emotion. The aching sensation way down inside me was quite real. I remember my first kiss. Wow. I didn't know anything about real love and it was still fascinating.

Because this man (Solomon) had done so many good deeds, had helped so many people, his name was like a healing balm all by itself. The mere mention of his name made people feel better. The ones that are pure and untarnished by the world naturally love such a man as this. Some of you girls may remember thinking so much of a man that you just kept writing his name and saying it, and writing your name with his name and putting your first name with his last name and then saying it and writing it over and over. You were getting the idea. Even the sound of his name is exciting.

The girl is smitten and calls to the man and says draw me. Pull me to you. I find my enjoyment in you. When it is all said and done, your love is what I will remember. This love we have is what is important, it's what we will look back on fondly. It is not the money, the things, the parties etc. It is this love that is making life wonderful. It is only right to love you.

Then the girl remembers how she must look to him. She recoils in horror at the thought that perhaps he won't think she is all that great. She says to him that she has been working and hasn't paid much attention to herself. But she can be pretty. She says don't look at me now, I'm a mess. Let me get fixed up and then you'll see. She wants to put her best foot forward. Then she asks him where he will be. Her plan is to get herself all fixed up and go find him. He says if you don't know where I am, follow those who are following me and you'll find me.

Now he changes the direction she is heading in by starting to compliment her. (vs. 9) He says she is actually quite pretty. Her cheeks, her hair etc. looks good to him. Verse 11 is the big change in her plans however. He says he will fix her up and it will be better than she could imagine. He will make her royal, complete with gold and silver. She will literally be the best that she can be.

That is the simple love story God gives us so that we might grasp the idea of what it is all about.

He tells us that the best emotion is love. No debate, no second opinions. He explains that when we look back on our lives we will understand. The problem is that we need to understand the purpose of our lives and the things that truly enrich us up-front in order to live a great life.

Our God knows that we will tend to be distracted by all sorts of things and therefore spend our lives doing meaningless and unimportant things. He knows we can spend a great amount of our time watching TV, playing games, getting high, looking at things which hurt us, thinking fantasies that pull us away from Him, seeking money, things, power and the list goes on and on.

Think with me now. If the truth is that the greatest emotion and the point of our lives is love (and it is) and we spend all our time doing meaningless and unimportant things, it should come as no surprise at the end of our lives, that when we look back on our lives, they were meaningless and unimportant. What a tragedy. This is why some old people are so bitter.

The horrible truth of being at the end of your life is that you cannot do it differently. The life you lived is all you have. How sad to then realize that you missed everything that was important. How can this be prevented? God so loves you that He gave you the answer. He wrote a book that will guide you if you will but let it. His intent is that your life be full, abundant and joyous. That sounds like a much better life doesn't it? Isn't it amazing that He says in his bible that Jesus came for this express purpose? [10]The thief cometh not, but for to steal, and to kill, and to destroy: I am come that they might have life, and that they might have it more abundantly. [11]I am the good shepherd: the good shepherd giveth his life for the sheep.

Wait a minute. He not only says that He came that you might have life and have it more abundantly, but that there is an enemy that you have that is out to kill you. You have an adversary that wants to steal and destroy your life. Keep thinking with me. If your enemy can get you to focus on all the things that are meaningless and unimportant, he can literally steal your life. The full, joyous life that Jesus wants you to have would be destroyed. Your very purpose for being here would be killed, or at the very least it would be maimed, mutilated, twisted or perverted.

Don't let that happen. Let Jesus kiss you with the kisses of His mouth. His love is better than anything. Picking up in verse three the name of Jesus is the name that is above every name. There is healing in the name of Jesus. Those who are pure love Jesus.

Once you see this Jesus clearly, once you understand anything of His love wherewith He loved you, once you realize that He literally gave His life for you, you too will call to Him to draw you. You will rejoice to run after your Jesus. You will be starting to realize that these are the times you will look back on fondly. These are the times of love. It is only right to love Jesus.

At some point in this scenario it will become evident to you that Jesus is remarkable and worthy of all the best of everything and you are woefully lacking pretty much across the board. It will occur to you that Jesus might not like what He sees when

He sees you. You have some fixing up to do. You want to make a great impression on your King of Kings. So just like the Shulamite girl you ask where you can meet Him later after you get more presentable.

The King's answer is absolutely remarkable. Listen to this wisdom. For those who wish to see Jesus, for those who truly want a loving relationship with Him, but are maybe having trouble seeing Him in His glory because they are so confused, messed up, un-pretty if you will. Jesus offers this advice: Follow those who are following me. You get with others who love Jesus and you'll find Him. That's true. That sounds like a good reason to go to church doesn't it? It's almost like He planned it that way. Yeh.

Look at verse 9 now. Jesus goes a step further and proclaims that He thinks you are pretty beautiful right now. Stop dead in your thoughts. Your God is telling you something awesome. He doesn't think the way you do. He doesn't count beauty the way you do. But He is God. He made everything didn't He? Yes. Listen to the bible in Colossians 1:13-19. Who hath delivered us from the power of darkness, and hath translated us into the kingdom of his dear Son: [14]In whom we have redemption through his blood, even the forgiveness of sins: [15]Who is the image of the invisible God, the firstborn of every creature: [16]For by him were all things created, that are in heaven, and that are in earth, visible and invisible, whether they be thrones, or dominions, or principalities, or powers: all things were created by him, and for him: [17]And he is before all things, and by him all things consist. [18]And he is the head of the body, the church: who is the beginning, the firstborn from the dead; that in all things he might have the preeminence. [19]For it pleased the Father that in him should all fulness dwell;

Jesus, who made everything, who is before all things, in whom all the fullness of the Godhead dwells, says you are beautiful. Wow!

He must see something you don't see. Right again. He sees past all the things that are unimportant and meaningless and sees the real you. He sees the you that is seated with Him in heavenly places. ⁴But God, who is rich in mercy, for his great love wherewith he loved us, ⁵Even when we were dead in sins, hath quickened us together with Christ, (by grace ye are saved;) ⁶And hath raised us up together, and made us sit together in heavenly places in Christ Jesus: ⁷That in the ages to come he might show the exceeding riches of his grace in his kindness toward us through Christ Jesus.

Jesus knows how dead you were in sins and trespasses. He loved you even then. He looks forward to a loving relationship with you that will never end. And then He goes another step forward. He says that He can fix you up better than you can fix yourself. He explains the difference is that He will use the truly precious things like silver and gold to frame you. You will be a beautiful treasure for Him forever. His point is that He will make you truly beautiful far surpassing anything you could do without Him

Think of it this way. It is His way of telling you that without Him you can do nothing. You can do all things through Him who strengthens you. You will never be what he created you to be unless you come to Him and let Him fix you up.

What do you respond to this? This is so important and life-changing that at first we are simply stunned. We have spent so much time on our selves doing meaningless things it is hard to grasp. The Shulamite had the same problem. Her response sheds a little light on it for us. ¹²While the king sitteth at his table, my spikenard sendeth forth the smell thereof. ¹³A bundle of myrrh is my wellbeloved unto me; he shall lie all night betwixt my breasts. ¹⁴My beloved is unto me as a cluster of camphire in the vineyards of Engedi.

When, as far as I was concerned, God was in heaven and minding His own business and seemingly paying no attention to me, I was all I could smell (verse 12). It was all about me. The purpose for my life was me. My favorite song was "Happy Birthday To Me". What's in it for me was my only concern. But then (verse 13) I got a whiff of Him. I sensed there was a smell much greater than my own. The more I smelled Him, the more

I loved Him. Now He is everything (verse 14). It's not about me, It's about Him. It all starts to make sense. He created me to love Him. I am for Him. It's all about Jesus. When I am with Him everything smells right. It is as it should be. It is as He intended it to be. It is wonderful!

Jesus then goes off again on how beautiful your eyes are (verse 15). You respond about how beautiful He is. This is a true love affair. He loves you. You love Him. The relationship is growing. It is like the great outdoors. It is blossoming on every front. It is on a rock solid foundation. This house that Jesus builds will stand the test of time. Glory!

I don't know about you but this makes me feel like shouting. This is so much greater than winning a football game or something like that. What my God is saying is that IF I STICK WITH HIM I WIN AT LIFE. There aren't really words that can express the joy that this brings. So go ahead and shout.

# CHAPTER 5

## *Nothing Special?...Think Again.*

### Chapter 2, Song of Solomon

¹I am the rose of Sharon, and the lily of the valleys. ²As the lily among thorns, so is my love among the daughters.

³As the apple tree among the trees of the wood, so is my beloved among the sons. I sat down under his shadow with great delight, and his fruit was sweet to my taste. ⁴He brought me to the banqueting house, and his banner over me was love. ⁵Stay me with flagons, comfort me with apples: for I am sick of love. ⁶His left hand is under my head, and his right hand doth embrace me. ⁷I charge you, O ye daughters of Jerusalem, by the roes, and by the hinds of the field, that ye stir not up, nor awake my love, till he please.

⁸The voice of my beloved! behold, he cometh leaping upon the mountains, skipping upon the hills. ⁹My beloved is like a roe or a young hart: behold, he standeth behind our wall, he looketh forth at the windows, showing himself through the lattice. ¹⁰My beloved spake, and said unto me, Rise up, my love, my fair one, and come away. ¹¹For, lo, the winter is past, the rain is over and gone; ¹²The flowers appear on the earth; the time of the singing of birds is come, and the voice of the turtle is heard in our land; ¹³The fig tree putteth forth her green figs, and the vines with the tender grape give a good smell. Arise, my love, my fair one, and come away.

¹⁴O my dove, that art in the clefts of the rock, in the secret places of the stairs, let me see thy countenance, let me hear thy voice; for sweet is thy voice, and thy countenance is comely. ¹⁵Take us the foxes, the little foxes, that

spoil the vines: for our vines have tender grapes. ¹⁶My beloved is mine, and I am his: he feedeth among the lilies. ¹⁷Until the day break, and the shadows flee away, turn, my beloved, and be thou like a roe or a young hart upon the mountains of Bether.

The Shulamite girl says she is just one of many. Nothing special, just a rose in the plain or just one of the lilies of the valleys. There are thousands of lilies in the valleys. You can't even count all of them. What difference does one more make anyway? The king corrects her. To him, she is like a lily among thorns. She stands out in magnificence. Do you see it? Yes there are billions of people in the world. What difference could you possibly make?

On your own, you aren't special, just one of many. You now have a choice.

You can just be one of many or you can be special for the King. Verse 3 is the key.

The girl sees the King is unique. She yields to him. She literally is going to sit in his shadow and be overjoyed to do it. He is the boss. He calls the shots. This is called submitting. Amazingly, this makes her very happy. She is not looking out for Number one, but rather says it is not her will but his that should be done. His fruit tasted good to her. Remarkably, she says what she got out of it was better than what she could have gotten on her own.

Think back to the end of chapter one. Remember, He is everything. It's all about Jesus, not you. This new information is pushing you further ahead. Keep putting it all together. God is telling you that on your own you are nothing. He is the one that counts. But He has been saying He can make you beautiful, He can make you special. You simply let him lead. His will not yours. He calls the shots in your life. Amazingly, this will make you happier than trying to do it yourself. The fruit He brings tastes good. That means what will come from this union between you and your God will mean something. It will have a purpose. It will be sweet.

In the story, the king brings the girl to the party and shows her off. He tells everyone that he loves her. Do you think that made her feel good? How would you feel if the most important person in all the world brought you to the big gala event and then told everyone that he loved you? I watched a husband being interviewed on television tell how his wife met George W. Bush (President of the United States) in Indianapolis. He said here was the most powerful man on the earth meeting his wife. Talking to his wife. That impressed him and he wasn't even the one meeting the president. Think how she felt. She was on television with the most important man on earth. Now consider this. The President was just talking to her for a few minutes. He didn't tell anyone that he loved her (I'm hoping). He is just a man. The God who made everything and controls everything (including the President), wants to tell the whole world that He loves you. His banner over you is love. That should take your breath away.

It took the Shulamite's breath away. Look at verse five. She says I'm about to faint, give me something to steady myself, give me some food or something. I am just lovesick. She is experiencing that emotional high that is overwhelming her. She is not sure what to do and how to react. She is lovesick. At this point, he is intimately loving her. And she loves it.

The word of caution is appropriate now. (Vs.7) Love must not be misused or abused. You cannot rush love. It must be in God's time. It is always as He pleases. Since the emotion of love is so strong, it is desired universally and our adversary knows we want it. We all have a strong tendency to love and be loved. We want it so badly that we try to force the emotions. We see what we like and feel this must be it so I'm going for it. The devil specializes in lies. He will fake love to ruin us. Satan knows that if we will fall for the lie, we may never find true love. There is a value to this love that God sees. Our enemy doesn't want us to know this. He lies to us trying to cause us to throw real love away and settle for a cheap substitute.

God gave me a great illustration of this when I was just a young man of about 20. It was Christmas time and I couldn't decide what to get my mother for Christmas. I was walking by Rost Jewelers in Glendale shopping center in Indianapolis when a clerk from the store asked me what I was doing. I told him I was looking for a present for my mom. He said why don't you get her one of these Hummel Christmas plates. It was the first plate in a series beginning in 1970. He said she would love it and it would grow in value every year as a collector's item. I said ok and bought it.

The next year I was walking by the same store and the same clerk said the same thing. I bought the second plate in the series. The next year I decided that I was not giving my mom a plate every year for the rest of her life. The years went by. Mom moved to Florida and more years went by. One day mom was walking by a collector's store and noticed the 1970 plate in the window. The price tag on it was $1500. She went in and questioned the clerk about it. Yes, that was a great buy because it would only go up in value. No, mother wouldn't buy it for she had one already. It was the ashtray on her living room table. That's right she was using that $1500.00 collectable treasure as an ashtray. What do you think she did? Right. She went home and gently cleaned it and hung it on the wall.

What was different about the plate? Nothing. What had changed? Mom now realized the value of that special, unique, first in a series plate. Years later, as I taught a teen Sunday school class, God brought it all home to me. We so desperately want to love and be loved that the devil lies to us and tries to make us take the most valuable thing we have (which is us) and use it like an ashtray. He can't make us an ashtray he can only try to get us to use ourselves as an ashtray.

You are more valuable than that. You are special, unique, one of a kind.

You have the ability to give the spouse God intends for you the greatest gift in your power to give. You. Think about this. No one on the face of the earth will get a gift like the one you give. The value of your unique body, soul and spirit is so immense that Jesus died for you. He thought you were worth that much. We can't even imagine how valuable that is. Don't use it like an ashtray. The real joy is in being the person God wants you to be and blessing the lives of those He intends for you to bless. What an abundant, overflowing with goodness and joy, smile-bringing, love-tingling present you will make. Make sure it is God's way and it will be great.

Our God tells us all about this so that we will not be fooled. We are to trust Him who will withhold no good thing from those who love Him.

The Shulamite hears the voice of her beloved just as we are to listen for and hear the voice of our beloved Jesus. Verse 8 is loaded with information by the very words that God uses. Let's look at them.

[8]The voice of my beloved! behold, he cometh leaping upon the mountains, skipping upon the hills.

First things first. We must hear His voice. He who has ears to hear let him hear. So many voices in this world. So many opinions. Who do you listen to? This could be the biggest problem all of us face. The problem is complicated by our biggest fault. Our biggest fault, our biggest obstacle to success and happiness is that "we think we think pretty good". We make decisions based on what we think will make us happy or be fun or exciting and really give us goose bumps of joy. The hang-up of course is that we are so often wrong.

I am reminded how I was about to kill myself. I had reached the end of the line. My way didn't work. No matter what I planned it just didn't turn out like I thought it would. It all seemed so different when I made my decisions. How could I have been so wrong? In retrospect, a much better question is how could I ever have thought that I knew what was going on. The realization that we have been duped, lied to, taken advantage of, just gave me an ache in the pit of my stomach. It literally made me sick. My personal devastation was overwhelming me. My hope was gone. I mean after all, if you can't trust *yourself* who can you trust. Where do you turn when your past decisions of where to turn turned out so wrong?

Turn to the one who planned it all. Turn to the one who knows why you are here. Listen to the one who loved you so much he died for you. Listen to your beloved.

My beloved comes leaping upon the mountains, skipping upon the hills. The thought here is one of closing a net. My beloved is bringing it all together. He is strong, swift and overcoming all obstacles—easily. He like a young strong, swift hart is bringing her to himself. She sees him through a partial wall, like looking through a lattice. She can't see all of him. She only sees glimpses of his glory. Oh but what she sees is exciting. He is alive, strong and wonderful.

He is talking to her, right to her very heart. Rise up, let's go, it's time. This altogether lovely one loves her, wants her and thinks she is beautiful. Listen to him as he explains it's time. The cold winter is past, the dismal rain is over and gone; the flowers are springing up and the birds are singing. It's as if all of nature is saying BE

ALIVE. The time has come for you to see why you were ever born. The time of your life is here. Come with your beloved.

In verse 14 he urges her to hold nothing back. No lattice anymore. He wants no secrets between them. He wants her to really open up and be with him, talk to him. He loves her. He loves her looks, her voice, all of her. In verse 15 he pleads with her to get together with him and between them to take away everything that would ruin their relationship. They are just getting started like tender young vines. They should protect their love.

She exclaims joyfully "my beloved is mine, and I am his and he is visiting me as one who feeds among the lilies. He is tending me, caring for me. She asks him to continue loving her, protecting her, throughout the long night until the dawn of a new day when she will see clearly and not be looking at shadows. "Bether" means separation. She wants him to do as only he can and close the mountain of separation between them like a deer going up and down the that mountain. He does it easily, swiftly. Closing any separation or division between them is easy for him. She gives him the green light. She wants him in her life. She wants his protection and readily admits she doesn't see clearly what is going on. She knows he is not bothered by the shadows. They are no problem for him. That's one of the reasons she is so glad that she belongs to him. She will lean on him forever.

Now think about this as you and God. Your God loves you. He loves to see you and to hear your voice. He asks you to hold nothing back. He wants you to have no secrets. He wants you to really live—to BE ALIVE. He cautions you to protect your relationship. Together with Him you will get rid of everything that would ruin your love. Your beloved is yours and you are His. He tends you, or as we would more likely put it, he takes care of you. He will continue taking care of you, protecting you and loving you until you can see clearly—until the night and all its darkness gives way to light and eternal life. Your God can easily close the separation and division that your sin has caused, just like a strong, swift roe goes up and down the mountains. Yes He will protect you until the light of life shines like the sun throughout all eternity. Where the veil will be removed and the darkness and shadows flee away and as the song says "you'll understand it better bye and bye".

# CHAPTER 6

## *There Will Be Night Seasons.*

**Chapter 3, Song of Solomon**

[1]By night on my bed I sought him whom my soul loveth: I sought him, but I found him not. [2]I will rise now, and go about the city in the streets, and in the broad ways I will seek him whom my soul loveth: I sought him, but I found him not. [3]The watchmen that go about the city found me: to whom I said, Saw ye him whom my soul loveth? [4]It was but a little that I passed from them, but I found him whom my soul loveth: I held him, and would not let him go, until I had brought him into my mother's house, and into the chamber of her that conceived me. [5]I charge you, O ye daughters of Jerusalem, by the roes, and by the hinds of the field, that ye stir not up, nor awake my love, till he please.

[6]Who is this that cometh out of the wilderness like pillars of smoke, perfumed with myrrh and frankincense, with all powders of the merchant?

[7]Behold his bed, which is Solomon's; threescore valiant men are about it, of the valiant of Israel. [8]They all hold swords, being expert in war: every man hath his sword upon his thigh because of fear in the night. [9]King Solomon made himself a chariot of the wood of Lebanon. [10]He made the pillars thereof of silver, the bottom thereof of gold, the covering of it of purple, the midst thereof being paved with love, for the daughters of Jerusalem. [11]Go forth, O ye daughters of Zion, and behold king Solomon with the crown wherewith his mother crowned him in the day of his espousals, and in the day of the gladness of his heart.

Our Shulamite girl is in the night season. We can look at it as her dreaming of losing her man. It's a nightmare.

We can also see this a tough time in her life. She is alone and she is afraid. (vs.1) She decides to go out and look for him. She longs for him. She aches to hold him close. He is nowhere to be found. (vs.2) The watchmen of the city find her wandering about and inquire as to why. She pleads with them to help her find him. (vs.3) After a while she finds him. O how she hugged him. She brought him home and into the chamber where her own mother conceived her. It is as it should be. All is well. It is true love and it is very good.(vs.4)

He is to her all that she could hope for. He looks good, he smells good. (vs.6) When she is with him it is peaceful and safe. She has never felt so secure. It is like there are protectors all around her making sure that no one can stop her love with her King. They secure her and all the luxury surrounding her. The trappings of a King are everywhere. It is rich, valuable, pleasurable, wonderful and hers. The best part is that it is all founded and held together with love. (vs.7-10)

O daughters of Zion, behold King Solomon. He is taking his place as the King and also my lover. It is all the way it should be. His mother approves. My mother approves. It is very good. (vs.11)

What a great love story! O yes and so much more!

Look at it now as the bride of Christ. God is telling us that there will be night seasons in our lives. There will be the times when it seems like our God isn't there. We can't seem to see him. We feel all alone and we are afraid. What should we do? Look for him. Ask for help in finding him. Understand that He is always there even during those dark hours when the shadows hide our sight. Don't lose hope. In just a little while He will come into clear view again.

Realize that, just as you ache for your lover, it is right that you yearn for your God. When you come together again it also is spectacularly special. O how you will hold each other. It is the way it is supposed to be. Think about it. It is why you were ever born in the first place. (vs.4) Yes, loving the Lord your God is the primary purpose of your life. God wants that intimate relationship with you.

This world, the flesh, and the devil will twist and pervert you with the intent that you will never know true love. If you jump for anything but God you are settling for, at best, second best. It is sad that for many of us we have trouble loving correctly because of all the things we incorrectly labeled as love. We lust, we seek pleasure, we use others and things- ever learning and never able to come to the knowledge of the truth. We simply do not even know that we don't know. Despair is right around the corner.

There is a better way. God's way. If you are reading this it is not too late. The father of lies will tell you that it is too late. It's time you stop listening to the lies. Your God, like a gallant King riding in from the wilderness (like out of nowhere, like coming in from the smoke, He becomes clearer) is starting to shake up your world. At first you hardly know much about him. You can make out an outline and you know he is something and as he gets closer you realize he even smells great.

Your God wants you yearning for Him. When you finally get intimate it is wonderful. You see why you were born. You realize he has all the power and he is in total control. Wow! The one who really is something loves you. You never felt so alive, peaceful, safe and secure in your life. And then he tells you that you will live forever. You have already passed from death unto life. This gives new meaning to eternal life. You get to be in love and be loved forever. Forever and ever and ever. "Wow" seems so inadequate.

It is all as it should be. It is all as it was planned to be. It is pure and right and marvelous in his sight.

# CHAPTER 7

## *Tell Me Again How You Love Me.*

Chapter 4, Song of Solomon

[1]Behold, thou art fair, my love; behold, thou art fair; thou hast doves' eyes within thy locks: thy hair is as a flock of goats, that appear from mount Gilead. [2]Thy teeth are like a flock of sheep that are even shorn, which came up from the washing; whereof every one bear twins, and none is barren among them. [3]Thy lips are like a thread of scarlet, and thy speech is comely: thy temples are like a piece of a pomegranate within thy locks. [4]Thy neck is like the tower of David builded for an armoury, whereon there hang a thousand bucklers, all shields of mighty men. [5]Thy two breasts are like two young roes that are twins, which feed among the lilies. [6]Until the day break, and the shadows flee away, I will get me to the mountain of myrrh, and to the hill of frankincense. [7]Thou art all fair, my love; there is no spot in thee.

[8]Come with me from Lebanon, my spouse, with me from Lebanon: look from the top of Amana, from the top of Shenir and Hermon, from the lions' dens, from the mountains of the leopards. [9]Thou hast ravished my heart, my sister, my spouse; thou hast ravished my heart with one of thine eyes, with one chain of thy neck. [10]How fair is thy love, my sister, my spouse! how much better is thy love than wine! and the smell of thine ointments than all spices! [11]Thy lips, O my spouse, drop as the honeycomb: honey and milk are under thy tongue; and the smell of thy garments is like the smell of Lebanon. [12]A garden enclosed is my sister, my spouse; a spring shut up, a fountain sealed. [13]Thy plants are an orchard of pomegranates, with pleasant fruits; camphire,

with spikenard, 14Spikenard and saffron; calamus and cinnamon, with all trees of frankincense; myrrh and aloes, with all the chief spices: [15]A fountain of gardens, a well of living waters, and streams from Lebanon. [16]Awake, O north wind; and come, thou south; blow upon my garden, that the spices thereof may flow out. Let my beloved come into his garden, and eat his pleasant fruits.

When it is as it should be, when it is true love, when it is as God planned it, it will be intimate.

Imagine you are the young girl in our story. Your King is also your lover. His family approves. Your family approves. It is pure and right and as it should be. He begins to compliment you on your beauty. That's good. He uses scenery common to the country back then, but the point is the same.

He thinks your eyes are gentle, loving, beautiful, altogether wonderful to gaze into. When he sees those big dove eyes framed by your luxurious, cascading, gently swaying hair and tells you about it you can feel his excitement grow. His excitement for you. That's good.

He is admiring every part of you. Your teeth are clean, white, and inviting to him. We see a little humor here in that he mentions they are all there. Not one missing. That's good too. Those teeth are smiling from between lips most luscious. Your speech goes along with your mouth. You don't cuss or use foul language. No F bombs from your mouth. You are speaking beautifully.

He notices possibly the softest hair on your body. It is the little area just in front of your ears coming down from your temples. It is perfect. It is like a special treat within a treat.

He compliments you on how well you hold yourself. Even your posture is great. You have a regal bearing worthy of a King's attention. He knows many valiant men want you.

When he moves down to your breasts, they evoke an expression of true love. He is taking you completely. He is staying with you all night. He is drinking in all of you- your beauty, your scent, your body -all that makes you uniquely exciting. He sees you as you are and you are stunning. That's very good.

There is a problem however. You are increasingly aware of all your flaws. I mean after all, what happens when he sees how imperfect you are. Doesn't he realize that there are times when you are not so pretty. In fact sometimes you have been known to say some downright ugly things. In real life, you are not always loving. What happens when he sees the real you?

Uh oh. He is not going to miss a thing. He is not stupid. He will not be fooled. There is no way you are fit for this King. Eventually this bubble has to burst. Your real self will ruin this relationship.

You have underestimated your lover. He has already taken care of everything. He has made provision for you to rise above your faults. Listen to the basis for an eternal relationship.

You are all fair, my love; there is no spot in thee.

How can he say that? How can this be? He says come with him. "Come with me from Lebanon." He repeats it. Look from the top of Amana, from the top of Shenir and Herman, from the lion's dens, from the mountains of the leopards.

It will make sense as we look at the meaning of the words. Lebanon means white. Amana is firmness, solid. Shenir literally means peak. Herman means abrubt. Lion's dens are a place of violence. We remember Daniel being thrown into the lion's den. The intent there was for the lions to eat Daniel. God supernaturally protected Daniel to show us we could be protected too.

We also remember the early Christians that Rome fed to the lions. They died not having received the promise. They and us will get it, someday. The point is that God will deliver some now, some later but deliverance is on the menu. Our order is placed. It is coming someday. Leopard means stain by dripping. Now back to the story. Your King says your job is to come with him. He begins with you being white. Remember his first meeting and you said you were black from the work. You didn't want him to look at you until you got cleaned up. (chapter 1) You were a mess and it was obvious. Remember? Without him you were lost, wandering without hope, without purpose. He said he would take care of everything. He would make you borders of gold with studs of silver.

He was not looking at you as you see yourself (flaws and all). He was looking at you as he sees you- Cleaned up, white, without flaws beautifully glimmering in regal attire. He makes you suitable for a King. He does it all. You only need to come with him.

You begin by being made white. Our God is totally holy, totally pure. There is no way to be intimate with God and have any sin. There can be no spot or blemish. Sin kills. The word death means separation. When there is sin, there is separation. A totally holy God will separate himself from all that offends. Therefore we must start with no sin. Jesus died for your sins. He was separated for you. He takes your death and you get his life. At the moment you believe this you are made white-pure and without blemish.

He repeats this because this is so important. You cannot begin a relationship with your lover until the sin is gone. You must be made white. Once this takes place, you are on firm footing. As songs say you are on the solid rock, the rock of ages. Your foundation is not built upon sand. It will not flush away but rather will stand the test of time.

It all happens abruptly. In the moment you believe the record God gives of His Son, you are born again and made white and taken to the peak where you can see the big picture. You have been delivered from the violence of this world and entered into the kingdom of God where all things work together for good to them that love God. No matter how much you were stained, even if the stains were mountainous. Stain upon stain, filth upon filth can still be removed.

Put it all together. In a moment of time, abruptly, your King takes you from the habitation of violence to the peaks of purity. He literally takes you to the heights with himself. He sees you now as seated together with him in heavenly places. You are safe now. You have passed from death unto life. You are without spot or blemish. You are loved. Follow on the story.

In the movie "Jerry Maguire", the hero is trying to impress his girlfriend and she interrupts him and says "you had me at hello". The meaning there was that he no longer had to try and impress her, he had already won her heart. This is the same thought as vs. 9. Along about the time when she is thinking that she is not good enough and is flawed and what can she do to impress him, he says in effect "you had me at hello". Our God says he is smitten with us just as quick as we come to him and introduce ourselves.

So you see it really is as simple as coming with him. He says come and we say yes.

The rest of chapter 4 is a record of intimacy. The words used denote extreme closeness and love. Once we see that it is pure, right and as it was planned by God, we simply say yes. We move from the filth of this world to the purity of the heights of heaven. We are cleaned and clothed by our God. Vs 11 explains that at this point, our outside is so good that even our clothes smell great, but oh, inside how wonderful we are. Yes our God wants us, He desires us.

We come when he calls us. It just gets better. True love is truly remarkable. We no longer fear this world. We are protected and provided. We love and are loved. We get to experience all the pleasures of love and closeness with our lover. It is a fountain of gardens. The implication is that it never ends.

Vs. 16 ends this chapter with the girl saying the only adequate response to this lover of hers. She prays that she may be better for him. She wants to be more pleasing to him. She wants him completely and wants him to take her completely. She wants her lover to enjoy her.

I don't know about you but I don't think saying this is "very good" does justice to what I'm saying. There really are no words to describe how marvelous this is. No matter how screwed up we are, no matter the mountains of stains, we get eternal life, peace, love and purpose through Jesus. I think he deserves a better life than the one I'm living. I want him to be pleased with my love. I want to give him more pleasure. I want to put a smile on his face.

# CHAPTER 8

## Not Now...Wait, I Didn't Mean It.

### Chapter 5, Song of Solomon

¹I am come into my garden, *my* sister, my spouse: I have gathered my myrrh with my spice; I have eaten my honeycomb with my honey; I have drunk my wine with my milk: eat, O friends; drink, yea, drink abundantly, O beloved.

²I sleep, but my heart waketh: *it is* the voice of my beloved that knocketh, *saying*, Open to me, my sister, my love, my dove, my undefiled: for my head is filled with dew, *and* my locks with the drops of the night. ³I have put off my coat; how shall I put it on? I have washed my feet; how shall I defile them? ⁴My beloved put in his hand by the hole *of the door*, and my bowels were moved for him. ⁵I rose up to open to my beloved; and my hands dropped *with* myrrh, and my fingers with sweet smelling myrrh, upon the handles of the lock. ⁶I opened to my beloved; but my beloved had withdrawn himself, *and* was gone: my soul failed when he spake: I sought him, but I could not find him; I called him, but he gave me no answer. ⁷The watchmen that went about the city found me, they smote me, they wounded me; the keepers of the walls took away my veil from me. ⁸I charge you, O daughters of Jerusalem, if ye find my beloved, that ye tell him, that I *am* sick of love.

⁹What *is* thy beloved more than *another* beloved, O thou fairest among women? what is thy beloved more than *another* beloved, that thou dost so charge us? ¹⁰My beloved *is* white and ruddy, the chiefest among ten thousand. ¹¹His head *is as* the most fine gold, his locks *are* bushy, *and* black as a raven.

[12]His eyes *are* as *the* eyes of doves by the rivers of waters, washed with milk, *and* fitly set. [13]His cheeks *are* as a bed of spices, *as* sweet flowers: his lips *like* lilies, dropping sweet smelling myrrh. [14]His hands *are as* gold rings set with the beryl: his belly *is as* bright ivory overlaid *with* sapphires. [15]His legs *are as* pillars of marble, set upon sockets of fine gold: his countenance *is as* Lebanon, excellent as the cedars. [16]His mouth *is* most sweet: yea, he *is* altogether lovely. This *is* my beloved, and this *is* my friend, O daughters of Jerusalem.

This relationship is marvelous. The king is overjoyed to have his girl. All is right in the world. Eat, O friends; everyone rejoice and be happy with us. But....

Why do we do it? Why are we so selfish. Why do we move from this great love, joy and happiness to our selfish mode. All of a sudden our wicked heart decides we have a better way. In our story the lover comes to his girl— because he loves her and wants to please her and enjoy her as it should be. She is sleeping, so she says not now. She doesn't think it is that big of a deal. I mean after all, she is not saying I don't love you, I'll never sleep with you again or anything close to that. She is just saying NOT NOW. Come back later.

The more she thought of him, and the touch of his hand on her, the more she changed her mind. This could be one of those great love moments. The kind of spontaneous actions that yield tender memories so exciting to even think about after the fact. But oh, how wonderful it is to feel in the making! Yes she would open to her lover. Where is he? Imagine the horror to realize he was gone.

The sinking feeling in the pit of her stomach hit hard as she called out to him with no reply. How stupid could she be? He is her lover, her protector, her life. How could she reject him. What would she do without him? He is the king. Look at how great he is. Look at how beautiful he is. He doesn't need her at all. She is the one that needs him! Think of how he cleaned her up and made her beautiful too. What a horrible thing to have done to such a wonderful man.

She went looking for him. The watchmen didn't realize who she was, for the king was not with her. They hit her thinking she was a prostitute. That's why they took away her veil. She had rejected her true love. She had said no to the one that loved her. Now they thought she was filthy and selling her love to any who had the money.

Vs. 8 If any of you find my love, please tell him I am just sick about it. I love him so much. I'm sorry and I want him back. I am just sick over this. 'They answer her with a question: What is so great about your man? The Shulamite girl, the one who was nobody, with nothing before the king came, then just unloads with praise for her man. From his complexion, hair, eyes, lips, hands, stomach and down to his feet, there is no one like him. He is altogether lovely.

You can feel the yearning in her heart as her words pour forth. You can also sense her desire to apologize and love her man. She truly wishes she could go back in time and make the right decision to love him as he asked.

Imagine the King of Kings. He is not just a great man. He is God! Imagine He loved you when you were unlovable. He cleaned you up and made you somebody. He wants to love you and protect you. He wants to enjoy you. He wants you to love and enjoy Him. How dare you say no.

Don't you realize that without Him you can do nothing. Without Him you have no protection. You are alone and you will get hurt. Remember chapter 4:8 all you have to do is come when He calls. Remember how fulfilling it was to be with Him. He took care of everything and you knew He would love you forever. The only thing that could prevent this was if you rejected Him. If you refuse His love you are on your own. What a stupid, foolish thing to do. How dare you reject One who is altogether lovely.

The problem we have is that He is the one that picks the time of visitation. In fact, as we have seen, there are night seasons when we can't even get a good view of Him. We know He is there and we know He loves us, but in this world we will have tribulation. So when He decides to visit us in a special love relationship we must always open up to Him and love Him fully. The lesson is hard learned and painful but once we resolve never to refuse Him, the joy is exceeding and worth more than our effort.

Once again, we have met the enemy and he is us. This points once again to the hideous deceit of the low self esteem doctrine being put forth throughout our world. The devil knows that he can't stop the love of Jesus. His plan is to get us so selfish that we refuse it. It is only in retrospect that the selfish man can see what a foolish thing he has done. You do understand that that means he has already wasted the love, the life, the joy His God wanted him to have. The GOAL is low self esteem.

We should think less of our selves every day and more of God and others. We should prefer one another in love.

God said no man ever yet hated himself. God is not a liar. We believe the lies because we don't think them through. If you really had low self esteem, it would not bother you that the other person got the job, after all they must be better than you. It would not bother you that the girl or boy doesn't love you, after all, what is there to love. When you really love someone and want the best for them you would actually prefer that they love the one that is better for them. It would not bother you that you are not wealthy, after all, it is only right, you don't deserve it.

You see, when you think it through, you see that the reason these things are upsetting is because you so love yourself—you are selfish. The more selfish you are, the angrier it makes you. How dare they not give you the job etc. The extreme selfish state brings the thought: well if I can't have her then nobody will. And he kills the girl he supposedly loved. This is the same reason that workers go back and kill people they worked with. Kids go back and kill schoolmates and teachers etc.

What happens to a fire when you throw gas on it? Right. What happens to an extremely selfish person when you tell them they have to love themselves? When you tell them that deep down they are really good and they need to realize that? Right. What happens when they finally realize that the world does not revolve around them—and never will? When they lose hope that they will ever get the girl or the job or the money or the fame etc? You know what happens. You are seeing it on school campuses, worksites etc.

Why are these crimes getting worse and more prevalent? We have been teaching our children that the problem they have is low self-esteem. We are throwing gas on the fire. Until we stop this it will only get worse.

People are so selfish that they can't hold a job, keep a relationship, love anybody but themselves, or yes even train children in the way they are to go.

Every great saint in the Bible had lower self-esteem than those around them. Paul said: there is that dwelleth in me no good thing. Isaiah said: Woe is me, I am a man of unclean lips etc. Moses said he didn't think he was the right man for the job. Joseph was back-stabbed and thrown in prison and never complained. Look it up. ALL of them seemed to have lower self- esteem. They tried to esteem others not themselves. It certainly does teach us that the goal should be low self-esteem. We should strive to think more of God and others and less of ourselves every day.

We are never told to love ourselves. On the contrary, God pleads with us to love our neighbor as we love ourselves. The problem has never been to love ourselves because we do that naturally. The problem is to love others. The first commandment is to Love the Lord thy God. He commands this because it doesn't come naturally. Think it through.

So the only thing preventing our happiness is us. The only thing we have control over is us. Hey, this is like a light at the end of the tunnel. Putting it together, God made us so that we can love Him and be happy. We have control to do that. Isn't that an eye-opening, amazing thought. We really can do all things through Him that loves us.

# CHAPTER 9

## *You Make Me Feel Like Dancing.*

### Chapter 6, Song of Solomon

[1]Whither is thy beloved gone, O thou fairest among women? whither is thy beloved turned aside? that we may seek him with thee. [2]My beloved is gone down into his garden, to the beds of spices, to feed in the gardens, and to gather lilies. [3]I *am* my beloved's, and my beloved is mine: he feedeth among the lilies.

[4]Thou *art* beautiful, O my love, as Tirzah, comely as Jerusalem, terrible as *an army* with banners. [5]Turn away thine eyes from me, for they have overcome me: thy hair *is* as a flock of goats that appear from Gilead. [6]Thy teeth *are* as a flock of sheep which go up from the washing, whereof every one beareth twins, and *there is* not one barren among them. [7]As a piece of a pomegranate *are* thy temples within thy locks. [8]There are threescore queens, and fourscore concubines, and virgins without number. [9]My dove, my undefiled is *but* one; she is the *only* one of her mother, she *is* the choice *one* of her that bare her. The daughters saw her, and blessed her; *yea*, the queens and the concubines, and they praised her. [10]Who *is* she *that* looketh forth as the morning, fair as the moon, clear as the sun, *and* terrible as *an army* with banners?

[11]I went down into the garden of nuts to see the fruits of the valley, *and* to see whether the vine flourished, *and* the pomegranates budded. [12]Or ever I was aware, my soul made me *like* the chariots of Amminadib. [13]Return, return, O Shulamite; return, return, that we may look upon thee. What will ye see in the Shulamite? As it were the company of two armies.

She praises her man as altogether lovely and the others want him too. It is only natural. They ask her where her man is so they can see this marvelous man.

My beloved is checking on his garden. He will do the necessary duties as an owner. He enjoys what is his. I am his! I am his and he is mine. Oh what a relationship. We are lovers and he enjoys me. He feeds on me.

The king now speaks words of love that she just melts to hear. He thinks she is beautiful. Tirzah means delight. Yes, he delights in her. When he says she is terrible as an army with banners he means that she is notable, conspicuous, she stands out. Oh yes, he noticed her in his garden and he likes what he sees.

Once again he applauds her beauty. However, what is notable here is not what he says but what he doesn't say. This passage is just like chapter 4 with the striking exception of verse 3. This immediately draws our attention to question what he left out and why. He left out "thy lips are like a thread of scarlet, and thy speech is comely". Why? Recall chapter 5 verse 3. She had spoken badly to him. She told him, not now. In effect she told him to go away.

Now he lets her know that he knows she used her lips and voice selfishly, but he still thinks she is beautiful, and he still loves her. Wow! Not only is he altogether lovely, he is forgiving as well. This man is the complete package. The king is rich, handsome, passionate, caring and forgiving too.

Verse 8, There are many in the kingdom. There are many the king loves and protects. This Shulamite girl is notable however. She not only is special to her mother (as all children are), she is special to others in the kingdom. Others in the kingdom praise her along with the king.

Verse 10. Who is this woman that is breaking on to the scene as the morning sun? She is beautiful as the moon. She is pure as the sun. And yes, she is notable, conspicuous among those in the kingdom. She stands out among the many.

Verse 11. She goes down to his garden to see how everything is going. She wants to help him. She is there to make sure his garden is as he pleases. Is the fruit coming? Is everything according to plan? Before she even realized it, she was in the forefront of the fruit bearing. She was surrounded by the generous ones, the ones that were really bringing forth fruit pleasing to her love. (Amminadib means my people is generous)

Verse 13. The others (not the generous ones) wanted her back. They liked having her around. They knew the king fancied her. The king asks them what they see in the Shulamite. It is as the company of two armies. This is very hard to understand but is so good as to be supernaturally written.

We have a key here from God to help us understand it. The key is the first verse of Chapter 7. He calls her a prince's daughter. He refers to the joints of her thighs.

Now we put it together. She is the prince's daughter. Who was the prince that had something happen to the joint of his thigh? God is pointing us to Genesis chapter 32. In the second verse of chapter 32 Jacob realizes that God's host is with him so he names the place Mahanaim. Mahanaim means 2 camps or 2 bands. Jacob had realized that there was his camp and there was God's camp. His army and God's army if you will. Later in verse 7 He divides his people into 2 bands. Then in verse 25 the man wrestles with him and touches the hollow of Jacob's thigh and moves it out of joint.

In verse 28 the man renames Jacob to Israel because Jacob now, as a prince, has power with both God and man. In verse 29 Jacob asks the man his name. The man answers in effect, why are you asking my name? You know who I am. I am God and God blessed him there. In verse 30 Jacob calls the place Peniel because He realized he had in fact seen God face to face and lived.

Now back to Song of Solomon chapter 6 verse 13. The word for company means dance. We now know the 2 armies is Mahanaim. They want the Shulamite girl to return to them so they can see the dance of the Mahanaim.

Get ready. This is really good. What does all of this mean to us?

Chapter 6:1. We who believe in our King Jesus should be speaking so well of Him that others around us want to see Him. They want us to tell them where they too can find this altogether lovely King of Kings.

Verse 2. Jesus is checking on His church. He is enjoying his people. He is taking in the fruit of His family. He is also taking some of His family out of the garden and bringing them home. He calls it gathering the lilies. Remember she is just one of the lilies in the valley. There are others in His family. There are others in the family of God.

For the rest of this chapter I will speak as if I am the Shulamite. Please understand that if you believe in Jesus, if you are born again, You are the Shulamite too.

Verse 3. But praise God, I'm in the family. I am His and He is mine. He is right here with me. He is feeding me. He will never leave me.

He delights in me. He thinks I'm beautiful. Sure there are others in the family, but he noticed me. He says I am conspicuous. I'm one of a kind and He loves me. He talks about my traits, the things he thinks are beautiful about me. He knows I'm sometimes all messed up. He knows I fall short of His expectations, but he forgives me. He is a merciful God.

Verse 8. He repeats that I am not alone. There are many others in the family. But isn't it amazing that he points out that a child is special to their mother. I have been born again. I have been born not of the will of flesh or the will of man, but of God. God is my mother and God is my father. When I was crucified with Christ I was put to death, nevertheless I live. Yet not I, but Christ lives in me and the life I now live in the flesh I live by the faith of the Son of God, who loved me and gave Himself for me. Yes God gave me life and I am special to Him. I am unique in the eyes of my God.

Others in the family see that God loves me. They know I have a love relationship with my God. They also speak well of me. Who am I that I should stand out in the family of God? My God is the one that cleaned me up and made me pure. He is the one that makes me to shine like a light in the midst of a wicked and perverse nation.

My response to all of this is I will help my God. I will go and check on the family and see if all is well. Are they bringing forth fruit pleasing to my Lord? Is there anything I can do to help them? Pomegranites are the lifted up ones. Am I edifying the body of Christ. Are they growing and prospering? Am I helping to lift up?

Before I was even aware of it, I was running with the ones that gave. I was wanting to hang out with those that loved and were generous.

When you are helping, loving, edifying some people will want you around. People do like to see someone who has power with both God and man. They like to watch the dance of the Mahanaim. I want to be a better dancer. I want power with God and power with man. I realize that if I am to help man, I need power with God. Dance even when I can't hear the music, because the music is in me. Jesus Christ is in me. I want to dance for Jesus. I want to dance with Jesus.

# CHAPTER 10

## *Take Me, I'm Yours!*

### Chapter 7, Song of Solomon

¹How beautiful are thy feet with shoes, O prince's daughter! the joints of thy thighs *are* like jewels, the work of the hands of a cunning workman. ²Thy navel is *like* a round goblet, *which* wanteth not liquor: thy belly is *like* an heap of wheat set about with lilies. ³Thy two breasts *are* like two young roes *that are* twins. ⁴Thy neck *is* as a tower of ivory; thine eyes *like* the fishpools in Heshbon, by the gate of Bathrabbim: thy nose *is* as the tower of Lebanon which looketh toward Damascus. ⁵Thine head upon thee is like Carmel, and the hair of thine head like purple; the king *is* held in the galleries. ⁶How fair and how pleasant art thou, O love, for delights! ⁷This thy stature is like to a palm tree, and thy breasts to clusters *of grapes.* ⁸I said, I will go up to the palm tree, I will take hold of the boughs thereof: now also thy breasts shall be as clusters of the vine, and the smell of thy nose like apples; ⁹And the roof of thy mouth like the best wine for my beloved, that goeth *down* sweetly, causing the lips of those that are asleep to speak.

¹⁰I *am* my beloved's, and his desire *is* toward me. ¹¹Come, my beloved, let us go forth into the field; let us lodge in the villages. ¹²Let us get up early to the vineyards; let us see if the vine flourish, *whether* the tender grape appear, *and* the pomegranates bud forth: there will I give thee my loves. ¹³The mandrakes give a smell, and at our gates *are* all manner of pleasant *fruits*, new and old, *which* I have laid up for thee, O my beloved

Talk about dancing! How beautiful are your feet! So here is our heroine, a girl that has power with the king and with regular people. The king again tells her how beautiful she really is. She is like a work of art by a master craftsman.

He goes on about her physical attractions noting that all is lovely. She is truly put together well. In addition, verse 4, she holds herself well. She has a regal bearing, stately with good posture. Heshbon means reason or intelligence. Bath-rabbim means daughter of many people. Put it together and the king is saying she has Eyes of Intelligence by way of the daughter of many people. She is smart, and handles herself very well in any situation, with any people. This girl is no slouch. She is conspicuously fine.

She is a sight for the king to behold. As if she was a work of art in a fine gallery, the king just stands and looks at her. Wow! She literally is his delight.

The king wants to touch her, smell her, kiss her. He wants to love her.

What would be her reaction? Vs. 10. I am his and his desire is toward me. In other words, she agrees. Take me I'm yours. What is great about this is that he not only has her—he wants her. He is reaching for her because he desires her.

Now they are a couple. They are together. Let us go... The wording here is awesome. This is a permanent relationship. Let us lodge. We are staying together, living together. You take my hand and I'll take yours. Let's get up early, no point in wasting our time. No delays. Let's do the work together. Let's check and see how the family is doing. Is everything growing? I want to love you there. I want the whole world to know that we are in love. There is fruit from our union all around us. No act of love is forgotten. I have a lifetime of fruit stored up for you. It's all yours.

Now look at this whole scene again with the king being King Jesus and the girl is you (any member of the bride of Christ).

God tells you that you are put together very well. You are literally the work of a master craftsman. You are no accident. You are the way God made you. You did not form yourself in the womb. You did not choose height, hair color, etc. But you are responsible for how you use you. You should use reason and intelligence. You should have self-control and handle yourself well at all times in any situation and among any people.

You should have a regal, stately bearing because you are married to the King of Kings. You should expect your King to want to spend time with you. Expect him to want to be intimate with you. He wants you. You are not just in the family, you are wanted and desired and loved. Your reaction should be "take me I'm yours".

Now let's get the stuff done that you were born to do. You have the talents you have to do the things he wants you to do. And you will do it all together. Remember when Moses told God that if God didn't go with him he wasn't going. Now you are like Moses. It's you and God. Doesn't make any difference what the others do. They may spend no time with God. They may not even get to know Him. They may bring no fruit. Doesn't change your relationship at all. You and God are living together.

Is everything growing in your relationship? Are you bringing forth fruit?

Are you getting excited about your God? Right there in the world you live in are you shining like a light? Can others see that you love God and He loves you? There (in this world) will I give thee my loves.

Oh wow, look what comes from a great love relationship. So much fruit all around you. You can smell it. A whole life of fruit and it is for your God. You have a reason why you are made the way you are, and a purpose for your funny nuances. You are you for Him. And it works. Just look at the fruit.

I like to think of it this way. I am checking on the family to see if they are getting excited about their God. I am trying to show the love of God to those around me. On God's behalf I am trying to put a smile on their faces. An old Mahalia Jackson song had a line that went "live right each day and smile on your way, it don't cost very much". I found that it doesn't really cost anything. A whole lot of times you can cheer people up for no money. Sometimes just a smile is all it takes.

Come to think of it, They ought not to be able to wipe the smile off our faces. I mean think about it. We have one who loves us and wants to hold us and has all the power to protect us. He made us the promise that He is working all things out together for our good if we love Him. Oh yeh, we get to live forever. He will never leave us and He will work His work through us so we know it will get done. The fruit that we bring Him will last forever.

Sometimes, I have actually blown a kiss to God when He has brought forth fruit through me. I am blowing kisses to the One I love. I pray I may help someone and, when it happens, it's like saying this is for you, and I blow Him a kiss. You may think it's corny, but I feel so close to the One I love, and I think He is blowing kisses back to me. I sure do love that.

# CHAPTER 11

## *We Need Affection.*

Chapter 8, Song of Solomon

¹O that thou *wert* as my brother, that sucked the breasts of my mother! *when* I should find thee without, I would kiss thee; yea, I should not be despised. ²I would lead thee, *and* bring thee into my mother's house, *who* would instruct me: I would cause thee to drink of spiced wine of the juice of my pomegranate. ³His left hand *should be* under my head, and his right hand should embrace me. ⁴I charge you, O daughters of Jerusalem, that ye stir not up, nor awake *my* love, until he please.

⁵Who *is* this that cometh up from the wilderness, leaning upon her beloved? I raised thee up under the apple tree: there thy mother brought thee forth: there she brought thee forth *that* bare thee. ⁶Set me as a seal upon thine heart, as a seal upon thine arm: for love *is* strong as death; jealousy *is* cruel as the grave: the coals thereof *are* coals of fire, *which hath* a most vehement flame. ⁷Many waters cannot quench love, neither can the floods drown it: if *a* man would give all the substance of his house for love, it would utterly be contemned.

⁸We have a little sister, and she hath no breasts: what shall we do for our sister in the day when she shall be spoken for? ⁹If she *be* a wall, we will build upon her a palace of silver: and if she *be* a door, we will enclose her with boards of cedar. ¹⁰I *am* a wall, and my breasts like towers: then was I in his eyes as one that found favour. ¹¹Solomon had a vineyard at Baalhamon; he let out the vineyard unto keepers; every one for the fruit thereof was to bring a thousand *pieces* of silver. ¹²My vineyard, which *is* mine, *is* before me: thou,

O Solomon, *must have* a thousand, and those that keep the fruit thereof two hundred. ¹³Thou that dwellest in the gardens, the companions hearken to thy voice: cause me to hear *it*. 14Make haste, my beloved, and be thou like to a roe or to a young hart upon the mountains of spices.

Our Shulamite girl loves her man. She wants to show him affection but there are others that would look down on her for this. In the culture of Israel at that time it was appropriate for family members to be affectionate and kiss and hug in public. It was not so for a man and a woman. So naturally, our heroine wishes her man were her brother so she could touch and hold him and no one would think it wrong.

How things have changed! How different is America in the 21rst century. Now we can't touch our own children lest someone think we are perverted. The simple affection of humans is being looked upon as evil. Kissing among family members is all but gone. We throw away natural affection and expressions of love and yet we flaunt unnatural lust and immorality. Women dress to attract the lust of men. All to often we see acts of sex performed in public and no one is ashamed.

I remember going for a walk in Israel next to the sea of Galilee. I was walking toward a park and saw in the distance what appeared to be a double date. Two couples were at the park. One person was laying flat on the ground with another apparently massaging her. The other couple was at the swing set with one in the swing and the other standing next to her, touching her back and hair much as a man would with his girlfriend. As I drew closer I realized that it was not two couples but rather it was four girls.

I was taken aback at first because they really acted like people in love. I talked with them for some time. They were in love. They were all girlfriends in the right and proper sense of the term. There was nothing inappropriate. They loved each other and they had natural affection and touched each other as God intends for all of us. They were in high school and they spoke four languages, English obviously very well. They spoke of going into the army when they graduated high school.

They said that they would find their husbands in the army. I told them that in America we do that in college. That is an interesting cultural change too.

As I walked away from them I pondered how different the cultures were. I was saddened realizing that the devil had stolen natural affection from us in America. By watching those girls touch each other and care for each other I realized we all really need that. Children need to be kissed, but maybe adults need it more. I'm not talking about sexual kisses. Adults need affection as an expression of human love. It's not about wanting to have sex with everyone, but rather they need to know people love and care about them.

We have twisted and perverted yet another of God's great gifts to us. People need people. People need contact—touching. It's not wrong, it's right. I go to retirement homes and the people are starved for affection. I visit people in the hospital and see they are starved for affection. They tell me that one of the worst things for AIDS patients is that no one wants to touch them. They are starved for affection. Good, clean, wholesome affection. Think of the many people who have not been kissed by anyone in years - maybe never. How tragically sad.

It becomes evident that we are being robbed and we don't even realize it. Possibly the greatest treasure we possess is our ability to love. We are being programmed to only have sex. Talk about missing God's best! Understand that love is what makes us different from the animals and plants. We have free will to choose to love. How bad is it when we only choose sex? We are completely missing the point.

There is however, the sex. There is nothing wrong in the correct context. Note our girl in verse 2 is now referring to going back to her house and in a private setting giving herself fully to her husband. It is good, clean, wholesome and right. In fact, in verse 3 she says this is the way it should be. And then the caution again, make sure it is the right person at the right time.

The others speak in vs. 5, asking who is this that is coming up and leaning on her beloved. The girl replies that this was always the man intended for her. From his birth he was meant for her.

In vs. 6, she implores him to love her (heart), protect her (arm) and never let her go. She notes that his love is as strong as death. There is nothing that can separate her from him. He is jealous for her. He is passionate for her. His love is a burning fire. Nothing can stop it, floods can't quench it or kill it.

But love also cannot be bought. In fact if a man tried to buy it he would be utterly looked down upon. Apparently love is rather special. True love is a powerful thing. Ironically, it seems everyone seeks after money, and what everyone needs is love, and money can't buy love. There is probably a riddle in here somewhere.

So what is the sum of the matter? Take it from the beginning. Her brothers go back to when she was a small girl, before she had a woman's body. They ask, what shall we do for our little sister when she starts to become a woman. Well that all depends on her.

If she is a wall—closed up, pure and letting no man in, we will honor her, reward her and exalt her as it should be.

If she is a door, —a loose woman opening up and giving entry to men before it is time, we will shut her up. We will be ashamed of her and there will be no rewards. We will want no one looking upon her.

Our girl is truly a heroine. She says: I am a wall. Yes I have breasts and you can see that I am a woman, but my breasts are like a tower. You can see my shape but no one is touching them but my husband. Then she was as one that found favor in her man's eyes. The king liked that. She was his and his alone.

Baalhaman means Lord of a multitude or possessor of a multitude. Solomon had lots of vineyards and lots of gardeners. Some even paid him for the right to tend his vineyards. They would then keep a portion of what they brought forth.

The Shulamite realized that she only had one thing to give Solomon. But this one thing was hers to give. Solomon says that others in the gardens hear her voice, but he wants to hear it too. She only has herself to give and he wants her. This book ends with her saying to him that she wants him too. She wants him to come to her quickly. Note in Revelation 22:20, this Bible also ends with Jesus saying "I come quickly". Our response, like the woman and John, should be "even so, come Lord Jesus".

Now we get to the heart of this book. This is the final chapter of the love story between Jesus and us. We, at least all of the born again Christians, are the bride of Christ. Let's see how God sums it up.

First, we should be affectionate with our God. We should want to hug him and kiss Him. It is only right. That is the way it should be. This world will never understand it, and that is ok. It's ok if the world looks down on me for loving Jesus. I am giving myself to Him completely anyway. My answer to Him is: "take me, I'm Yours".

The world says who is this coming up out of the wilderness, leaning on her beloved. The Gentiles are coming up out of the wilderness, leaning on Jesus. We saw Him coming from Israel, that is who brought Him forth. Jesus came as a Jew, was born a Jew, lived as a Jew but praise God He took a Gentile wife.

This Gentile wife says Jesus set me as a seal upon your heart. Love me with your perfect love. Set me as a seal upon your arm.

Protect me, fight for me, hold me and never let me go. Death will not stop your love for me. As a jealous husband, you will not allow any to take me away from you til death do us part. Since I live forever with you, I will always be with you. I am never going to die. You have given me eternal life.

Your love burns fervently. I may not be passionate at times, but you always are. Nothing can stop your love. The waters can't quench your fire for me. Strong waters cannot drown or in any way dampen or kill your love.

The intimacy we have cannot be forced. No one can force love. No one can buy love. If one were to think they could buy love, that thought alone shows they don't understand love. MY GOD IS LOVE. When I am holding onto Jesus I am holding love itself. Pure, holy, wholesome, altogether wonderful love.

So what would be my advice for a small child just starting out on life's road? If you will stay pure. If you will be a wall. If you do not open to every Tom, Dick or Harry that comes by, you will not regret it. Your life will be rewarded with true love. You will find favor with God. Your God will exalt you, love you, hold you and make you fruitful. Yes, your union with your God will be fruitful.

People love winners. You will be a winner. Some will want to pull you away, but you are a tower. You will be seen but not touched. Your Jesus likes that about you. You will be His.

Sure, there are lots of others in the family of God. You can only give yourself. But you are yours to give. You can choose to walk with Jesus. You can choose to be intimate with Him. You can talk to Jesus. He wants to hear from you. Sure there are others talking with Him, but He specifically asks to hear from you. He actually loves you. When you realize who it is that loves you your reaction should be: even so, come quickly, Lord Jesus.

# EPILOGUE

My prayer is that you see how marvelous this Jesus is.

That you believe the record God gave of His son. That Jesus is God and loved us so much that He took upon Himself the form of a man. As a man He lived a perfect life. He did not deserve to die. Then, as a man, He chose to die for our sins so that we might live together with Him forever. He said that whosoever believeth in Him should not perish but have eternal life.

Think about this love He has for you. He would rather die than have you live in darkness now and burn in a lake of fire for eternity. He really is the lover of your soul. He really is the only hope you have.

I believe in Jesus. I love Jesus. I hope you do too. Always remember, God Wrote It To You.

written with love for you,
Chris Ray

# PERSONAL REFLECTION OR GROUP STUDY QUESTIONS

The following questions are intended for personal application. The intent here is for personally applying the teaching of Scripture to your personal life.

I recommend going through these after every chapter. You are encouraged to come up with your own questions as well.

Whether you are alone or in group study, the value of meditating on God's word and how it relates to you is vital to your life.

Really thinking about your life and its meaning will help you immensely. Keep in mind that if you spend all your time doing meaningless and unimportant things, when you get to the end of your life and look back, you will find your life was meaningless and unimportant.

God wants your life to be abundant, full of purpose and meaning. Remember, happy has always been the plan. Also note: if Jesus is the King of Kings and the Lord of Lords,( and he is), if he has all the power and is everywhere, (and he does and he is), if he is in you, how can you not be great? <u>So your first question:</u>

How is your life now?

# Questions and thoughts for "What's your purpose?"

1. Sometimes we are treated unfairly and rude by our friends or even our family members. They say unfair things about us and spread false rumors. *If one of these friends should happen to ask for our forgiveness for the wrong they have done, can you easily forgive them?*

2. Do you realize that you have treated Jesus unfairly, yet he loves with a perfect and unfailing love? Do you realize to gain his forgiveness all that you have to do is ask?

3. Does this kind of love help you love and befriend others that have treated you poorly?

4. Other thoughts to ponder as you read this book. Think on these questions now and write your thoughts under each question below. You can ponder these thoughts again at the end of the book.

5. Why are you here?

6. What is the reason for your life?

7. Why are we all here?

# Questions for "The greatest Song of all".

1. What is your favorite love song?
2. Why?
3. How does it make you feel?
4. Do you have a favorite love story?
5. Why?
6. How does that make you feel?
7. Do you think that Song of Solomon could become one of your favorite love stories?
8. We are bombarded by all kinds of images on TV and in magazines that try to sell us things using beautiful people. When you see these advertisements, how do they make you feel?
9. The author of this book said Jesus loves you even if you do not think you are beautiful and he loves you no matter what you have done. *Jesus loves you unconditionally. How does it make you feel to think that someone loves you no matter who you are and what you have done?*
10. How do you love others? Is your love unconditional?
11. Do you have any examples of your unconditional love?
12. You can begin today to love more like Jesus. Name some concrete ways to start.

# Questions for "Nothing Special?...Think Again".

1. Do you ever feel like you are just a number, one of many at school or work?
2. How does it feel when someone in a group of people gives you a complement or even gives you a reward?

   The author says that the Shulamite woman feels she is not special, that she is just ordinary. If she were a flower in the field she would not be noticed, because she is only one little flower out of thousands. However, the King says, she is the most radiant flower in the garden. "A rose among thorns"

3. How do you think the King made the Shulamite woman feel?
4. The real King of the Universe is Jesus! He wants you to feel loved and beautiful not just ordinary. You are not just a number to Jesus. He wants you to have life and have it more abundantly. Are you ready to have a love relationship with Jesus?
5. The author told of a story about a valuable collector's plate he bought for his mother. When the mother thought the plate was just a normal, everyday plate what did she do with it?
6. Once she found out that the plate was worth a lot of money, what did she do with it?
7. What was different about the plate? Had the plate changed at all?
8. So why was she treating the plate differently?
9. You have always been valuable just like the expensive plate. Are you treating yourself like the ashtray or the extremely valuable plate?

The author wants us to feel loved and accepted because Jesus loves us and accepts us. However, he gives us a warning to live our life "God's Way and It Will be great!"

10. What happens when we make decisions that are not based on biblical principles?
11. Are there things in your life that cause you to make poor decisions?
12. What can you do to help make decisions that will keep you close to God?

# Questions for "There Will Be Night Seasons".

1. Ever have a nightmare? When you awoke were you still afraid?
2. Think of your greatest love. Now He's gone. Scary isn't it.
3. What do you do when you are afraid?
4. When you went through a tough experience who or what did you seek to find peace and security?
5. What do you do when you cause the problem that brings the night season?
6. What do you do when you are confused and can't seem to see the way to go?
7. Have you ever really sought out God? Really looked to see Him?
8. How did it turn out?
9. The author says "Your God wants you yearning for Him. When you finally get intimate it is wonderful. You see why you were born. You realize He has all the power and He is in total control.
10. Next time you go through a tough experience, do you think you can look to God to meet your needs? How will you go about that?

# *Questions for "Tell me again how you love me".*

The King in the story compliments the Shulamite woman. He thinks she is very beautiful in every way. The author says, "the king sees her as stunning." However, the Shulamite worked in the fields for her father and mother.

1. How do think the Shulamite woman felt about her appearance when she was with the King?
2. How did the King feel about the Shulamite woman?

   You can not have a relationship with God with sin in your life. "Our God is totally holy, totally pure. There is no way to be intimate with God and have any sin."

3. It is impossible for us to be pure on our own. How does the author say we can become pure before God so we can have a relationship with Him?

   The author says, "Jesus died for your sins. He was separated for you. He takes your death and you get his life. At the moment you believe on Jesus you are made white-pure and without blemish."

4. Have you asked Jesus into your heart so that you can have eternal life and have an intimate relationship with Him?
5. If not please take time and do it now.
6. Do you now feel clean and without spot or blemish? Why or why not?

   When the Shulamite woman realizes that the King loves her "she prays that she may be better for him. She wants to be more pleasing to him."

7. What do you do each day to have a better relationship with this Jesus who loves you?

8. Think of how spending time with God will make your life better. Dream of how it would be to always walk with God. The joy, the lack of fear, and the power of God with you always. Name the specific parts of your dream.

   List some of God's promises about what he will give you if you seek after Him.

9. Do you ever consider eternal life? What will it be like? Who will you be with?

# Questions for "Not Now...Wait I Didn't Mean It!"

1. Have you ever had a close friend that moved far away? How much did you miss them once they were gone?
2. In the story, the king came to his wife and she did not respond to him. Then, when she changed her mind, he was gone. How do you think she felt when she realized he was gone?
3. The author explains that people are naturally selfish. Like the wife, most don't consider others first. Many times Jesus may come to you when it is not convenient for you and ask you to do something for him. How will you respond?
4. What activities in your life get in the way of serving God? What is it that prevents you from loving God?

Think back to a time when you selfishly did what you wanted to do only to realize later that you had hurt someone you love. This could be a time when you didn't do what someone else wanted because you didn't want to.

5. How did you feel when you found they were upset? What could you have done differently? Did you ever really want to turn back the clock so you could do right?
6. Without turning back the clock, how did you make it right?
7. What have you lost because of your selfishness?
8. What makes you think you have any rights?
9. Would you forgive others who behave selfishly toward you?
10. The author said that we "are never told to love ourselves. On the contrary, God pleads with us to love our neighbor as we love ourselves." Who do you love as yourself?
11. How are you investing in a true love relationship with God? What are you putting in the relationship?

# Questions for "You Make Me Feel Like Dancing".

Here is an interesting thought. The author says "She praises her man as altogether lovely and the others want him too. It is only natural. They ask her where her man is so they can see this marvelous man."

1. What was the king doing?
2. What does it mean when the king says she is "terrible as an army with banners"?
3. What did the Shulamite think her man thought of her?
4. Where does the Shulamite girl go? Why?
5. Is there anyone who delights in you? How do you know?
6. Is there anyone that you delight in? How do they know?
7. What are some ways to express your love or delight in others?
8. Do you have power with God? How do you know?
9. If you have power with God, how do you use it?
10. Do others love your friends just because they love you? This would be the 'Any friend of yours is a friend of mine" thinking.
11. Do you feel like dancing? Why or why not?

# Questions for "Take me, I'm yours!".

1. What makes you you? That's right, what is so special about you?
2. List traits that make you unique. If you had a lover, what would you like to hear them say to you?
3. Who cheers you up?
4. Who do you cheer up?
5. What are some of the ways you could cheer others up?
6. Do you long to give yourself totally to the one you love? Why or why not?
7. Is there someone who wants to give themselves totally to you? Why or why not?
8. Are you being the greatest "you" that you can be? If not, what will you do about that?
9. What types of work are your abilities suited for? Since God made you, it is reasonable to assume he made you suitable for certain types of jobs. What are your dreams and visions of the future?
10. Where does God fit in your workday? Where does He fit in your leisure and play time?

# Questions for "We need affection".

1. Have you ever seen someone else being affectionate and wished it were you?
2. Do you consider yourself an affectionate person? Would others?
3. What are acceptable ways of showing affection? Do you?
4. What types of behavior would be considered inappropriate outside of marriage?
5. Why?
6. Do you feel like you need affection—someone to show you they care about you?
7. How would they show you they care?
8. How would you respond?
9. Do you feel there are people around you that are starving for affection? Why or why not?

The author says, "Please understand that if you believe in Jesus, if you are born again, you are the Shulamite too." Below is a chart giving some examples of how Christians are like the Shulamite woman.

The author says, "Please understand that if you believe in Jesus, if you are born again, you are the Shulamite too." Below is a chart giving some examples of how Christians are like the Shulamite Woman.

| She Loved King | King Loved Her | Christians Love Jesus | Jesus loves us |
|---|---|---|---|
| She want to serve King | King wants to give her riches | Christians want to serve Jesus | Jesus wants the best for us |
| She talked about the King | King talked about her | Christians talked about Jesus | Jesus hears and likes it |
| She wanted to be close to him | He wanted to be close to her | We want to be close to Jesus | Jesus wants to be close to us |
| | | | |
| | | | |
| | | | |
| | | | |
| | | | |
| | | | |
| | | | |
| | | | |

How many examples can you give where Christians and the Shulamite woman are alike? Write them down in the Chart.

As you end this study write down your feelings on this topic of love.

1. Is your life going to be better because of love?
2. Are you going to make someone else's life better by loving them?

If you are not married, you may want to list the traits you are looking for in a mate.

If you are married, you may want to list the traits that your mate may like seeing in you. Talking to them about this might be a good opening step.

3. Do you want to love God? Tell Him. Read the Bible and learn all about Him. Try to be the person He would like you to be.
4. How can you show the love of God to those around you?
5. How can you live so that others want to know the God you love?

# The Last Question:

In light of all you have just studied, do you see why there is so much confusion and twisting of the truth concerning love and sex?

Hint: Love is so important to everyone that humans have a tendency to lie, cheat and steal to get what they consider love. Only too late do they realize that they did not have love, they just had sex. Sex is a cheap substitute for love. Real love is in a class all by itself. When sex is with true love, it is right. And those who have it know it.

There is a force for evil in this world that lies. The lies are abundant regarding love. You don't have to look real hard to see the broken lives, misery and sorrow in the wake of those who believe the lies. The evil wants people to get so caught up in the lies that they never see the truth.

The truth is: God so loved you that he gave His only begotten son that if you would believe in Him you would have eternal life.

# THE SIMPLE GUIDE

The simple guide to learning who God is and loving Him is tried and true.

Just one example of this happened at the Hamilton County Jail.

I was walking in to lead a bible study when I was stopped by an inmate who was sweeping the floors. He asked me if I was the guy who said "read a chapter a day until you die". I said that sounds like me.

He said he had been doing that for about a year and a half. Then, in a highly excited voice, he said "man that works".

The reason that works is God. God honors you for honoring Him. If you show you will listen, God will talk. Think about it. The God who has all the power and is everywhere and knows what is going to happen tomorrow will talk to you.

God is the one who came up with this idea. He wrote the book for us to know Him. To know what He likes and doesn't like. He gave His Son that we might be with Him. This wonderful love relationship is His idea. He can make it happen for you.

God wrote it to you.

A simple guide for those who want to be part of the greatest love story of all time.

At the risk of making this too formal (and hence taking out the spontaneity and excitement factors) I will give a step by step guide to moving into a love relationship with Jesus.

1. Understand that you probably believe numerous lies already.
   a. For example, one is that this won't work for you.

2. Read the bible.
   a. Read at least a chapter a day until you die.
   b. Ask the God of the bible to explain it to you.
   c. Don't spiritualize or symbolize it.
   d. Just listen to what God is saying
   e. Ask God how this applies to you.
   f. Expect Him to speak to you.
   g. Look for the God of the bible in the bible.

3. Hang out with God's people.
   a. That's right. Go to a bible believing church and get involved.

4. Tell God you want to love Him.
   a. You need to know Him better.
   b. Take the time to talk to Him.
   c. Listen to Him.
   d. Enjoy Him

5. Love Him.
    a. You make the choice to love Him.
    b. Look for ways to show Him you love Him.

The truly great thing about this relationship is that there is room for others. Tell others how great your love is. Go ahead, brag on Him.

If you would like to tell me your story, go to cray@iccbpi.com and leave me your comments.

CPSIA information can be obtained
at www.ICGtesting.com
Printed in the USA
BVHW061202081122
651442BV00003B/163

9 781953 791511